C000096618

Love, Sex
& Marriage

LOVE, SEX AND MARRIAGE

An Hachette UK Company
www.hachette.co.uk

Summersdale Publishers Ltd
Part of Octopus Publishing Group Limited
Carmelite House
50 Victoria Embankment
LONDON
EC4Y 0DZ
UK

www.summersdale.com

Printed and bound in the Czech Republic

ISBN: 978-1-78685-535-0

Substantial discounts on bulk quantities of Summersdale books are available to corporations, professional associations and other organisations. For details contact general enquiries: telephone: +44 (0) 1243 771107 or email: enquiries@summersdale.com.

RELATIONSHIP TIPS

Love, Sex & Marriage

FROM THE VICTORIANS

PENELOPE SHAFTESBURY

summersdale

Introduction

The Victorians were a curious bunch, weren't they? Outwardly obsessed by respectability, restraint and propriety, yet inwardly brimming with emotion, longing and lust. To be sure, they faced many of the same romantic dilemmas that we do, and they can still teach us a thing or two. This illustrated collection of unusually candid advice is intended to preserve their pearls of wisdom for the benefit (and maybe also the amusement) of latter-day lovers.

Ladies, be sure to ascertain
the size of your potential
husband's bank balance before
you betroth yourself to him.
Failing that, do ensure his
endowments show promise
of substantial growth.

A little theatrical feigning
of a headache may induce
in one's spouse the most
agreeable keenness to
be wantonly pleasured.

If your partner invites you to attend a certain type of party, indulge them, however peculiar the apparel you may be obliged to wear. All things considered, you may have a jolly good time.

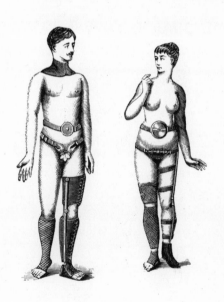

Post-coital ablutions
are of the utmost
necessity, unless you
want your bedmate to
endure an egregious
olfactory infraction.

The hourglass figure is perennially fashionable for ladies and all the more achievable with the use of a sturdy corset. Take care, however, not to pull it so tight as to break the glass and spill the sand, as it were. Your kidneys will thank you.

A well-kept moustache
ensures a more willing
and satisfied partner
when disporting oneself
in the bedroom.

In a woman, as well
as a man, a good, firm
grip ensures that your
interaction begins
strongly, promising full
and frank intercourse.

Ladies may engage in the appreciation of the male form, but it must be discreet: a small pair of binoculars affords the ideal means of locating prime specimens in the park – as well as the perfect birdwatching excuse: 'Why, sir, I was merely admiring the peacock!'

If traditional, demure
methods of eliciting male
attention fail to furnish the
requisite results, a flash
of dainty ankle is apt to
bring the suitors running.

Modern technology will now permit a husband and wife to create photographic erotica — for either their own private enjoyment or for sharing among friends of very liberal and like-minded disposition.

In the absence of a
gentleman's truncheon,
the smooth shaft of a
stout candle may serve
as a means of achieving
bodily satisfaction for
ladies of any age.

After a particularly exertive session in the bedroom, it is prudent to ride side-saddle to lessen one's pelvic discomfort.

A bride may demonstrate
her facility with a blade
upon the wedding day
itself, thereby giving her
husband an unmistakeable
signal that she is not
to be trifled with.

Following a night's festivities, some stains of an intimate character may not yield even to the expertise of a seasoned washerwoman.

A husband must never
excite the jealousy or
suspicions of his wife
in his interactions
with staff, particularly
those of the female and
flirtatious persuasion.

Ladies: should a
gentleman suitor overstep
his mark, remind him
of his place with a swift
kick to the sternum.

A wife should practice
and perfect her look of
extraordinary disdain
for when her husband's
drink-sodden excuses are
particularly preposterous.

A young lady may set tongues wagging around town by the way she handles a stiff rod.

Gentlemen, it is a sad truth, but sometimes the bald-lipped man may steal the affections of your beloved. Cultivate your luscious whiskers nevertheless.

If one's wife happens to find a suspicious bill upon her husband's bureau, he must make haste to provide the most innocent explanation of his activities. 'The axle of the carriage needed that lubricant, my dear!'

Never allow your spouse
to leave the house with
anything on their face
apart from the look of
a deeply sated lover.

The back row in a darkened theatre is a prime location to engage in amorous tomfoolery. But if your date has dressed in multiple layers, you may find it rather a challenge to disrobe or probe them.

Upon closer inspection, many ladies that one observes about town are in fact gentlemen disguised as the fairer sex. This phenomenon of 'cross-dressing' is but a harmless outlet for natural expressive impulses and a wife should make her wardrobe available to any husband motivated to indulge this temptation.

The small ads in many a newspaper are often replete with coded messages placed by those desirous of indulging in some remarkable amatory practices. For instance, a housemaid may claim to be open to activities both upstairs *and* downstairs.

Ladies, your corset may
chafe somewhat, but the
sensation of tightness may
be found most agreeable
if your imagination is
allowed to conjure certain
scandalous scenarios.

Profound gratification in the bedchamber may be achieved by denying your partner their sight and proceeding to stimulate their unencumbered senses to the fullest extent.

A proud display
of millinery is an
unmistakeable signal that
one is very much 'up for it'.

Embrace those moments of intoxicated affection before the contempt of sobriety returns with the morrow and a vengeance.

During courtship, a lady may safely excite her suitor's desire with liberal use of suggestive phrases. She may yearn aloud for a 'pearl necklace' perhaps, or remark upon her most accommodating 'tradesman's entrance'.

The couple that rides
together thrives together.

A lady's parasol may
double as a weapon if
a suitor's lust threatens
to get the better of
him. Often merely the
brandishing of the
item, accompanied
by a devastating look,
will do the trick.

Be sure to lock
eyes with a potential
suitor before drawing
attention elsewhere
by fondling your
magnificent silky folds.

The size of a groom's feet
is reputed to give a fair
indication of the magnitude
of his gentleman's truncheon.
Brides may make the
necessary calculations
and mental preparations
for the wedding night.

Gentlemen, an oral douching before kissing in the French style will improve your chances of a repeat performance. Douche bags and pipes for this purpose may be obtained from any good pharmacy.

However ridiculous the
conceit of the white
dress may seem — given
the number of prior
conquests made within
a lady's bedchamber
— nothing else will do
for your special day.

Persistence can be
an admirable trait in a
seducer, except when the
odds are severely stacked
against you. Then you
are simply a horny fool.

Gentlemen, when marital relations take a turn for the worse, it is always prudent to revert back to the natural order of things.

Ladies, pretend to blush at his advances rather than admitting to the nauseating sweats occasioned by his clichéd and clumsy courtship.

Long hair is regarded as an indicator of health and fertility in a woman. Ladies, if your locks are lacking, weave straw or part of a dried bush into your scalp to arouse the attentions of men and the envy of other women.

Ladies, a word of caution regarding your use of fragrance — overzealous application is apt to send your suitor into a frenzy. Less is more.

In bed, a wife must
often have but one thing
on her mind: how to
avoid what is on his.

In the animal kingdom, the male often performs a courtship dance to attract his mate. In the world of men, however, a rhythmic display may invite ridicule. Gentlemen, if you want to remove her petticoats, retain your dignity.

Men appreciate prodigious
posteriors and they are
incapable of dissembling
upon the matter.

A little Halloween dressing up (or indeed, dressing down) may add a certain piquancy to proceedings in any relationship.

It is a truth universally
acknowledged among
painters that the ladies
soak their bloomers
for an artist. So, my
dear sirs, perfect your
perspective and refine
your impasto and you are
sure to enjoy her fast-o.

If you're interested in finding out more about our books, find us on Facebook at **Summersdale Publishers** and follow us on Twitter at **@Summersdale**.

www.summersdale.com